GW00400087

At The Centre of Time

To Ashley

At The Centre of Time

HARVEY WASSERMAN

AUBURN HOUSE

Published in 1995 by
Auburn House,
A division of Salmon Publishing Ltd,
Upper Fairhill, Galway
Reprinted May 1995

ISBN 1 897648 37 5

Calligraphy by Kirsten Hocking
Cover illustration by Sue Smickler
Cover design by Poolbeg Group Services Ltd
Set by Poolbeg Group Services Ltd in Goudy 11/14
Printed by Colour Books, Baldoyle, Dublin 13.

To Sarah

Contents

I AM ALIVE AND
I AM DEAD

THERE IS A FUTURE AND
THERE IS ONLY NOW

THERE IS A PAST AND
THERE IS ONLY NOW

I AM AT THE CENTRE
OF TIME

Time. Time. Time. Time. Confusion. We humans say there is time. Scientists say time is elastic. Time exists. Time does not exist. So all things happen now. All things that ever were happen now. All things that ever will be happen now. The open mind receives past, present and future. Professor Hawking tells us about time. But our confusion is not lessened.

The illusion of time is created for the soul's learning on earth. In the timeless, spaceless reality, the inexperienced soul finds difficulty in progressing. On Earth, the school for the retarded requires that information be absorbed in a linear fashion. In the timeless, spaceless reality where all knowledge is available simultaneously, the immature soul is confused, learns little that is useful.

The illusion of time on Earth is created for the immature soul to slowly perceive reality, to slowly absorb the lessons needed to be learned, to gradually move toward knowledge, toward pure light. It is as if a film were slowed to heighten perception of any evolution moving too swiftly on the film for clear understanding.

LIFE IS CYCLE
ILLUSION IS TIME
DREAM REALITY
ALL DIVINE

The creation of the illusion of time needed to promote the slow and careful learning of the immature soul requires the parallel creation of all life moving in cycle. Beginnings are endings. Endings are beginnings. Each facet of life, of creation, returning once more close to its beginning. In this repetition, in this beginning and return, learning by the immature soul is also enhanced. The perception of cycle simplifies process, simplifies learning.

The growing worship and preoccupation with the linear moves true learning away from the immature soul with parallax distortion. The worship and segmentation of time imprisons the immature soul, imprisons the immature soul away from learnings needed for advancement.

As the immature soul advances, the perception of time dissolves. The separation between realities dissolves to a learning, to a communion with the divine.

WHAT IS THERE
BESIDES LOVE

WHY DO I LOOK IN
ANY OTHER DIRECTION

MADNESS DIVERTS ME

TERROR BE DAMNED
I SURRENDER

Only love justifies life. Only love honors life. Only love sanctifies life. Only love at the center, at the core, of each life brings satisfaction, brings warmth, brings meaning to life. In the flow of Divine love, ego dies, terror dies. In the flow of human love, the heart, vulnerable and often racked in pain, retreats in terror. The ego in terror diverts itself with meaningless engulfing nonsense. The heart retreating in terror constructs a prison for its home. Retreat from the true task, diversion from the true task, is madness. The bird must not refuse to fly, the fish must not refuse to swim, or all is madness. Surrender to the task through terror, through pain. The warmth and bliss of love will find you.

I HAVE THE ILLUSION
THAT
I HAVE THE POWER
TO
COVER THE ILLUSION
OF MY UGLINESS
I AM A TIN GOD
ALIENATED
FROM
THE TRUE GOD

We are all fragments of the divine spark. Debased self worth, debased self-esteem, is illusion, a powerful illusion that haunts much of mankind. False teachings create this illusion. Separation from the Oneness creates this illusion. The journey of learning toward Oneness becomes twisted. The obstacles seem insurmountable, the valleys untraversible. Illusion can cover illusion – illusion of power, illusion of perfection, illusion of arrogance, illusion bathed in narcissism, illusion creating the fragile false image that we are God. First and foremost, heal the illusion of self negation. See your reflection of the divine spark. The journey of learning, the journey to the Oneness travels in ease, in joy, the obstacles vanquished.

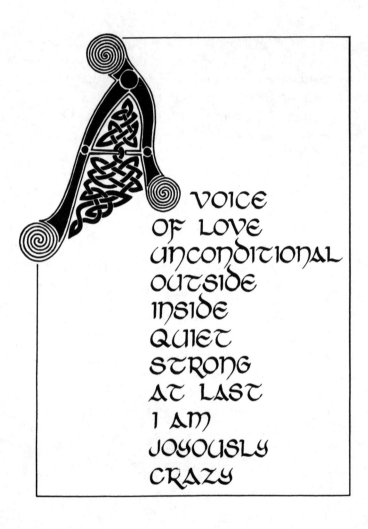

A VOICE
OF LOVE
UNCONDITIONAL
OUTSIDE
INSIDE
QUIET
STRONG
AT LAST
I AM
JOYOUSLY
CRAZY

The voice of God speaks to all of us in the quiet spaces of our mind, the quiet spaces between thought. Listen. Be guided. Be comforted. Find reassurance and peace. At that special moment, amplified by grace, the voice speaks strongly out of the quiet: Dance like David. Dance in joy before His Ark. You are no longer bound in saneness. You live at last. You live unbound in more than one reality.

NEAR DEATH EACH WEED IS BEAUTIFUL

The fear of death is the fear of life. We so fear death we must deny it, and so we deny life. so we deny beauty. Live each day on the knife edge of awareness between life and death, an edge shimmering in light and beauty. "It is a good day to die."

YOUR PUPILS
WILL
TEACH YOU
YOUR PATIENTS
WILL
HEAL YOU
YOUR DISCIPLES
WILL
ENLIGHTEN YOU

Guru, YOU ARE A DANGEROUS PERSON except for the briefest instant. How often the devotee is led away from finding the guru within. Seeker, never trust a guru even for the briefest instant unless the guru laughs a lot, unless the guru is humble, unless the guru is indifferent to your money, unless the guru finds joy in your leaving, unless the guru celebrates your transcending him.

ONLY A CONDUIT
HOSANNA
ONLY A CONDUIT
PEACE
ONLY A CONDUIT
CONNECTION
CONTINUITY
I HAVE PREPARED
RICHES FLOW THROUGH ME
NO GREATER JOY
ONLY A CONDUIT
ECSTASY

Prepare, and the mind vanishes. Prepare, ego's terror vanishes. Prepare, grey and black vanish. Prepare, and foolishness evaporates. The Divine cosmic flow hollows the body, streams through the cavity that preparation has prepared, connecting from all to all, the eddy of its current swirling graciously and gently in bliss, in ecstasy.

ALIVE
DEAD
A THREAD
PRECIOUS
UNIMPORTANT
BUT
FOR YOUR
LOVE

The immature soul in human body balances poised on a knife edge between life and death, a slender filament all that is necessary to move the body and soul toward death. In this delicate balance life glistens in importance. Death, appearing important to the ignorant soul, is unimportant. Only love transcends the dichotomy. The preciousness of life, the unimportance of death, are mere shadows in love's radiance.

I had this day
with pain
with tears
with love
with terror
with curiosity
with disappointment
with laughter
with uncertainty

But
I had this day

The soul on Earth, the immature soul, the retarded soul on Earth needs a multitude, a rainbow of experience. The soul in this school must be educated, must be re-educated by this multifaceted rainbow of educational experience. The soul on Earth perceives the experience in pleasure and the experience in pain as opposites – one to be desired, the other to be avoided, complained about and detested. Indeed this is a mistaken attitude, a mistaken learning. The pleasurable and unpleasurable tools of learning need to be equally accepted and appreciated. Indeed it is often in the fire of suffering that most progress and learning take place. The immature soul surfeited in pleasure often stagnates and deteriorates. The harmonious interplay, the counterpoint between pleasure and unpleasure can most probably produce the symphony of learning and enlightenment. The successful student celebrates all facets that each day brings and in that celebration moves in the music, carrying it to the Light.

A PERFECT GARDEN
CAPILLARIED WITH BRANCHES
CARPETED IN PERFECT WISDOM
PROTECTING, WITHIN ITS GREEN
SYMMETRICAL WALLS
THE GREAT STATUE RISES UP
REACHING OUT
CHRIST
BUDDHA
MOHAMMED
MOSES
I KNEEL
SURRENDER;
AS A CHILD
THE GREAT STATUE LIFTS ME UP
TO ITS BOSOM
TRANSFORMING THE WORLD
TO LIGHT

Perfect wisdom heals us. Perfect wisdom guides us. Perfect wisdom teaches us, sending us the great teachers to tell us what we already know, to tell us what we already know and do not listen. The great teachers open our ears to the inner voice.

The child in each of us knows. Surrender to the child. surrender to the knowledge. The arms of the teaching easily lift the child in loving transformation to the Light.

ROMANCE
DESTROYER OF LOVE
TOUCH ME
BUT
LIGHTLY

Angels play. Fairies play. Children play. As adults your play together in love restores joy and aligns the spirit with the joyous dance of angels, the joyous dance of fairies, the joyous dance of children. As adults on this Earth there is much to learn, much labor to perform, long journeys to travel, a gray and bleak journey without the lightness and colour of joy, without the dance of joy. It is a dance of joy whose platform is the true knowing of the other. As the dance becomes contaminated with illusion, illusion that in partnership the journey is completed, the individual passage to Light no longer needed, the platform shimmers in iridescent decay and crumbles to emptiness, torture, suffering. Play, dance, children, in the knowing, the true knowing, of each other.

Tears
Terror
helpless
I submit to the Doctors
technology penetrates
my heart

With tears
wails of Death
then
peace
bliss
warmth
Endorphins?
presences in my room
around me
their hands
no effort
move through my chest wall
no effort
making a change
protection ——————

In ignorance, in arrogance, the filament tilts me to the edge of death, no other lesson intense enough to free the ego imprisoned in ego. The time was not yet. The learning must be certain, profound. Their presence is made known, the lesson is complete, the lesson moving the immature soul from terror to peace.

MEN
RAISED AS RIVALS
MEN
RAISED FOR COMBAT
    AND STRUGGLE
LONGING FOR NURTURE
FROM EACH OTHER
AFRAID TO TOUCH
        HEARTS
MORE THAN OF DEATH
KILL EACH OTHER
AT LEAST A LITTLE

Men were once raised to love each other before they moved to the love of women. This is the natural order of things. Men loved men and brought this love to their women, their hearts strong and open, making women's hearts joyous. Machines came. Industry came, requiring man separate from man. Allegiance to industry, to machine, no longer allegiance to men. Men raised in the combat of industry, their arms and hearts struggling against each other to the glory of machine, men's hearts empty and sad in the longing, in the unfulfilled longing for other men. Men only look to their women in desperate love, indeed, unfulfilling love. The women's hearts cry and are sad.

Oh Mother
Oh Father
Oh Brother
Oh Sister
Oh Uncle
Oh Aunt
Oh Cousin

Teach the child
    to know who he is
Teach the child
    to know the world
Teach the child
    to know what is real
Teach the child
    to know what is of value

Oh Mother
Oh Father
Oh Brother
Oh Sister
Oh Uncle
Oh Aunt
Oh Cousin

Knowing who he is
    moves child to God
Knowing the world
    moves child to God
Knowing what is real, of value
    moves child to God

his journey flows
    on
your teaching

The journey, the road to Oneness moves forward on correct knowledge, on true learning, on transformation, on healing, on growth. The teaching of each child is holy vocation. False teaching requires much relearning, much healing. The journey is slowed, misdirected, even stopped. Correct teaching moves the infant to child, the child to teenager, the teenager to adult, the adult through maturity into the arms of Oneness.

POWER
OVER / INNER
SAINT OR SINNER
GOD OR THE DEVIL
WHICH IS THE ONE
YOU INVITE TO
DINNER?

There are but two paths to the Void – the path of love or the path of conquest. The path of conquest, seductive in its illusion of immortality, tempts many men. The path of conquest, seductive in its illusion of towering, overpowering oneness, tempts many men. The path of conquest, in cunning, in self-serving manipulation, armed with lies at the point of the sword, wins the allegiance of many men. The path of love, slow, difficult, patient, intermittently illumined in Light, the path of love, struggling toward self-knowledge of heart and mind and body, finds wisdom as it reaches arms outstretched in open heart toward its union with the Oneness.

I'm NOBODY
      DESPAIR
      EMPTINESS
      DEPRESSION
      VULNERABILITY
I'm SOMEBODY
      EXCITEMENT
      CONFIDENCE
      INVULNERABILITY
      FRAGILITY
I'm NOBODY AND
      I'm SOMEBODY
Ahh h   h

Man knows he is nobody, an insignificant grain of sand in an ocean of sand whose numbers are beyond counting. Man, in his insignificance, finds fear, despair, depression. Man struggles to somebodyness, a desperate struggle to find a fragile illusion of importance, of excitement, of uninvulnerability. Man in his nobodyness can discover that each grain of sand is unique and important, an atom, an essential part of the vast Oneness, finds peace and joy and bliss. Man in his somebodyness finds that in his essential insignificance he is a vibrational microcosm of holographic infinity, finds inner power, comfort, wisdom. In the paradoxical union of creation, nothingness and somethingness, the soul is complete.

HEARTBROKEN
BEFORE TIME
HEARTBROKEN
NOW
IN TIME
LIFE WANTS ITS END

LIFE LONGING FOR MORE
LOVE
A TREE
A BIRD IN FLIGHT
CREATIVITY
ENDINGS ARE BEGINNINGS
METAMORPHOSES IS HARD

Each man's heart vibrates synchronistically in union with man's agony, with man's suffering from the beginning of time. Each man's heart, amplified now in his suffering by the agony flowing through his past, flowing from the ages, longs for relief, for death. Each longing for death is a death. Each death an ending, each ending a place of beginning. Each place of beginning stirs hope in the heart, hope nourished in the blood of all life. Every seed must struggle mightily to burst through its shell to sprout.

TOUCH THE HEM
OF GOD'S ROBE

BEFORE BODY AND
HEART ARE PREPARED

YOU WILL BE CUT DOWN

Man is mind-body and man is spirit. Neither mind-body nor spirit functions alone. Mind-body without spirit is a putrefying lump of clay. Spirit without mind-body is a wisp of smoke dispelled by the most gentle breeze, is the thin shell of a balloon floating in apparent freedom until it touches thorn or rock to explode. Mind-body must be prepared. The greyness, the blackness, the olive green, the bloody red must be cleansed. Mind-body firmly planted on Earth tills the soil and rests, the outstretched arms of mind-body reaching upward toward the stars, toward the Universe, toward Oneness, providing a shelter, a protection, a path for the spirit.

NLY THE GODS
SEE
HOW ALL RELATES
WE MORTALS
CONFUSED
CAN ONLY LOVE AND
LAUGH ———.

Man is retarded. He cannot see. He cannot understand. Man is intelligent. He longs to see. He longs to understand. There is paradox and there is no paradox. Retarded man, limited, sees paradox. Intelligent man, longing for understanding, for paradox's resolution, struggles, succeeds and fails in frustration. The wise man accepts, laughs in the acceptance, loves in the healing. In our retardation, in our intelligence, we can love and laugh.

STAND ALONE
STRONG
UNDER YOUR FEET
THE EARTH IS YOURS
ALONE

STAND TOGETHER
GENTLY
THE DANCE OF LOVE
FROM EYE TO EYE
CONNECTS US ALL
NO LONGER
ALONE

Each man stands alone. The man who pretends otherwise is weak. The man who knows he stands alone is strong. Each man stands alone on his Earth, drawing strength from the ground, drawing strength in flexible union with the Earth. Each man in his aloneness stands in the flow of divine, cosmic love. Through each man the flow of divine, cosmic love creates an intertwining, endless web, a connection of love that transcends the separateness. Man, you are not alone.

YOU
MADE ME DIFFERENT
HOW I SUFFERED
ONLY TO LEARN
A GIFT WAS GIVEN ME

Differences belong to God, not to man. When differences, in self-delusion, move toward man, differences twist and writhe in torture, in agony. In the crucible of misdirected allegiances, awareness transmutes difference. Annealed in this fire, difference learns its true allegiance to the Divine. The star in the stone can now be seen in refracted light. The jewel knows itself.

FEAR MY FRIEND
NO GROWTH WITHOUT YOU
TO LIFE'S END?
WALK BESIDE MY COURAGE
TO JOURNEY'S END UNKNOWN
UNTIL
AN ANGEL COMES
THROUGH WISDOM'S EYE
AND HEALS MY HEART

Union with the Infinite severed at birth produces fear. Separate from the infinite the ego struggles mightily, futilely to deny its insignificance as it stands alone. Egotism, narcissism, arrogance are illusion hiding weakness, smallness, the knowledge of autonomous insignificance.

It is in the awareness of oneness with the Infinite that peace and bliss and significance are to be found. Life's journey is to move from the separateness of birth to the union of maturity. Many immature souls lose their way on their journey. The diversions, the pathways away from truth, are many. The journey towards truth, towards union, guided by angels can take many forms, the end result always the union with oneness, with the infinite, with God.

Remember that angels guide our way, radiant in love. Remember, angels have no wings, need no wings, only radiant projections of love's energy which can enfold the weary, frightened traveler.

I AM LOST
MORE THAN 1
        KNOW
UNTIL MY BEAR
RAKES MY THROAT
WITH HIS CLAWS
TO AWAKEN
ME

Children of Earth, you all know the truth. The great teachers have come again and again to remind you of the truth. To forget the truth, to ignore the truth, to put aside the truth, to live and move in life unguided by the truth generates pain, a growing pain increasingly difficult to ignore. Your minds, your bodies are designed to live in truth, to think in truth, to move in truth. The amorphous pain growing in size and ferment as truth is denied transforms itself to a giant beast whose clawed violence tears at mind and body.

I am a Vessel
I Fill the Vessel
I am Empty

I am a Vessel
Faith Touches Me
I am Full

In the Void, in the emptiness, in the nothingness of space is eighty percent of the energy of the Universe. In our emptiness we are attuned to the Void and the vastness of energy flows through us, is accessible to us. Ego is a mountain of nothingness. Emptiness permits communion with Oneness. In that communion the energy of nothingness is available. In that communion with the Oneness our insignificance brings us significance, brings us the peace of knowing our place in the order of things.

INNOCENT
BENEVOLENT
THOUGHT
BRINGS ME HOME
WITHIN THE
HOUSE
OF GOD

God has many homes within us. God's palace resides in the belly. In each man lives a saint. In each belly the saint within waits, waits for the palace doors to open, innocent, benevolent thought the lever, the latch permitting the palace doors to open. In innocent, benevolent thought they open to release the radiant, shimmering, golden light that illumines the man now called saint that illumines the world around him.

FIND BUDDHA
A BABY'S LAUGH
A BABY'S SMILE
FULL OF BELLY

FIND BUDDHA
WISDOM'S LAUGH
GENTLY SELF-MOCKING
IN SELF-ACCEPTANCE

LAUGHTER SHOWS
THE POWER

God laughed as He created the world. God laughed as He created the Universe. The soft, rounded belly the open door of God's palace, radiant in shimmering, golden light, bellowing in joy and laughter beyond intelligence, beyond meaning. The laughter beyond meaning brings meaning to existence. A baby's belly, a baby's matchless joy and laughter. The infant remembers.

God
Why
   is there suffering

Why
   is there terror

Silence
outside

Inside
a voice
distant
if only
   I could hear

Ask me
what
   is the task

I know
relieve suffering
relieve terror

Perhaps
I do hear

Man knows his task. The only task. He does not listen to what he knows. Instead he curses God. He questions God. He curses God in fury, "Why, God, is there suffering? Why, God, is there terror? Where, God, is Your compassion?" No answer. Some men speak for God, their voices thin and useless as a wind-broken reed. The curses rise up into the silence with mounting fury. God is murdered in men's hearts. Man turns instead to frivolous occupation. Man turns instead to inflicting greater suffering and terror upon man. Listen. There is only one task. Listen. The knowing voice is in you. The only task for man is the relief of suffering and terror. All else is foolishness. All else is degradation.

MY TONGUE CONNECTS
THROUGH GENERATIONS PAST
TO STAR   LIFE
REBORN

THE   TONGUE
IS A PLACE
TO ERASE
ALL
ILLUSIONS
OF
TIME
AND
SPACE

The reptiles knew. The reptiles knew from their beginning. The reptiles know in quantum awareness. The reptile is within us. Make friends with the reptile. Make peace with the reptile. Make contact with the reptilian. The quantum transducer is yours as you slip into reptilian skin, moving beyond time, beyond space, beyond the stars.

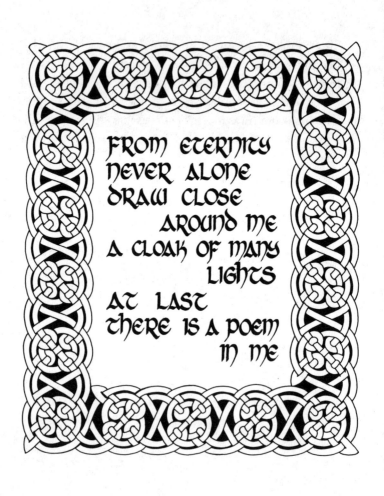

FROM ETERNITY
NEVER ALONE
DRAW CLOSE
    AROUND ME
A CLOAK OF MANY
        LIGHTS
AT LAST
THERE IS A POEM
        IN ME

What gift can man give to Divinity? Only painting, dance, music and poetry. The artist gathers round his light in ecstasy and returns the gift as poetry.

She comes to me
a girl with no soul
don't touch her
help her
suddenly
burning sulphur
inhaled
cold fear
nothing seen
everything felt
beyond my power
ENRAGED
I COMMAND YOU
in the name of
GOD
JESUS
MOHAMMED
MOSES
GET OUT OF HERE
YOU DON'T BELONG
my god there is a devil
but then there must be angels

The teaching came to me through the ages twisted by false voices, false writings, leaving me in the hands of logic, in the hands of technology, in the hands of science. The teaching must be relearned, recreated in blinding experience. The old becomes new. The presence of evil is felt and known, the fear of its presence transcending the fear of transforming my reality.

THE GREAT ACUPUNCTURIST
WITH BUT A SINGLE
NEEDLE
PUSHES THROUGH REALITY
BEYOND
TIME

All healers of any discipline move beyond art, move beyond science. All healers feel the energies, sense multiple realities. Carried on these waves, art and science transcend themselves.